In the Park

Written by Zoë Clarke

We can run in the park.

We can jump in the park.

We can hide in the park.

We can pedal in the park.

We can hop and skip in the park.

Talk about the book

Ask your child these questions:

1. Name three things the children did in the park.
2. What did the children pedal on in the park?
3. Why did the boy playing hide and seek put his hands over his eyes?
4. Do you know what the hop and skip game at the end of the book is called?
5. What do you like to do in the park?
6. Which activity from the book do you like the best?